RDS

Information Technology

A review of inspection findings 1993/94

A report from the Office of Her Majesty's Chief Inspector of Schools

London: HMSO

ISBN 0 11 350055 6

Office for Standards in Education
Alexandra House
29–33 Kingsway
London WC2B 6SE

Telephone 0171-421 6800

Contents

Introduction

This subject profile for information technology provides a review of the findings from inspection conducted for and by OFSTED during the academic year 1993/4. It continues the publication by OFSTED of subject reports focused on the quality of provision made for, and standards in, information technology in maintained schools. It extends information and discussion to include aspects of inspecting information technology which are of direct interest to inspectors and may be found relevant by schools and those who provide them with support and supplies.

The evaluation of standards, quality of education and provision for information technology is based on evidence from the inspection of 34 primary schools and 240 secondary schools. The secondary schools were inspected for OFSTED by teams led by Registered Inspectors, and the primary schools by teams led by Her Majesty's Inspectors of Schools (HMI) and usually containing independent inspectors in training.

In addition, evidence from the inspection of information technology and computing in primary and secondary schools by HMI was used to assist in the interpretation of patterns emerging from analysis of the main body of inspection data.

Too few IT and computing lessons were observed and recorded post-16 in the inspections conducted for OFSTED by Registered Inspectors to permit the writing of meaningful sections on standards of work and teaching. Similarly, the information offered on pupils with special needs was insubstantial, offering little with which to report trends in practice.

Subject Report

Main Findings

At all Key Stages information technology (IT) elicits interest and enthusiasm from boys and girls, and they co-operate readily and responsibly with one another in using it. Attitudes to work are generally very positive, and motivation to acquire relevant skills is high.

Standards of attainment in relation to capability at Key Stages 1–2 are largely satisfactory or better, but modest compared to overall standards in all subjects. Most pupils experience only part of the Programmes of Study (PoS) for IT capability; work in control and the applications and effects of IT is often missing.

In most primary schools IT is being marginalised, especially at Key Stage 2, because of other pressures and a lack of teacher expertise in the various aspects of IT. In most primary schools there is little teaching geared to help pupils to progress beyond their existing levels of attainment.

Standards in Key Stage 3 and Key Stage 4 have a similar profile to, but are rather below, corresponding aggregates for all subjects. Fewer high or very high standards are achieved in Year 10 in IT compared with other subjects and compared with IT standards in Year 11.

In Key Stages 3 and 4 pupils experience a wider range of applications of IT than in previous Key Stages, but also much practising of low-level skills. The quality of learning of IT through applications within the curriculum varies from good to poor in different subjects. Even where IT contributes to learning in a subject, its use sometimes adds little to pupils' IT capability.

Where there is no timetabled provision for teaching IT at Key Stage 3, and responsibility for developing IT rests entirely with different departments, there is frequently a mismatch between the intentions behind school policies and their operation in practice. Cross-curricular delivery of IT works only where subject teachers are also confident in IT, pupils' progress is monitored, and structures are in place for motivating and effectively co-ordinating delivery.

Where IT is taught as a separate module or stand-alone course, coverage of the PoS is more rigorous; but often there are insufficient opportunities to apply the IT skills so acquired to work in other subjects. Absence of such opportunities deprives pupils of the benefits of rigorous training.

Very few schools conform to the requirements of National Curriculum (NC) assessment and reporting of IT. Systems of recording and reporting are developing, but they mostly record experience rather than actual attainment; most teachers still lack the confidence to judge pupils' attainments in IT, nor is appropriate IT and professional training always available for them.

The development and support of pupils' IT capability depends on the commitment and expertise of too few staff in schools. The needs of such staff for training in teaching and assessing IT are rarely met.

Key issues for schools

Schools might wish to take particular note of the following key issues:

- More rigour is needed in meeting the requirements of the National Curriculum at all Key Stages, to ensure that pupils gain their entitlement to all aspects of IT capability. (Paragraphs 6, 13, 36, 38, 41)

- Teachers' competence with IT and ability to use it fruitfully in teaching need strengthening. (Paragraphs 20, 24, 28, 43–44)

- There is a lack of differentiation in teaching IT capability. Pupils' previous experience of IT and their interests need to be considered in planning the IT curriculum and the manner in which it is taught. (Paragraphs 29, 31)

- Progress has been made in assessing, recording and reporting pupils' IT capability. But much in-service training is needed to help teachers at all Key Stages to feel more confident in judging at what levels of IT pupils are working, and ready to utilise the outcomes of such assessment to inform subsequent teaching. (Paragraphs 33–35, 44)

- **In primary schools** specific discussion and teaching should be offered so as to extend pupils' understanding of, and competence with, major IT applications. Such teaching might form an integral part of the many fruitful opportunities pupils commonly have to apply IT. (Paragraphs 4, 21–22)

- The great variation in teaching IT capability in different classrooms in a primary school needs to be reduced. The headteacher or an IT co-ordinator responsible for developing IT capability needs to have adequate time to provide support for colleagues, and do more than attend just to the physical resources and software. (Paragraph 4)

- **Secondary schools** need to exercise care to ensure that their declared policy of teaching IT to Key Stages 3 and 4 operates as intended. A policy of teaching IT entirely through other subjects, or one of teaching IT as a subject totally divorced from subsequent application, would not normally, on its own, yield adequate coverage and rigour. (Paragraphs 10, 40–42)

- Effective co-ordination of IT in a secondary school happens where:
  - there is serious commitment from school management to make co-ordination work;
  - well-qualified, trusted, senior members of staff are charged with implementation and monitoring; and
  - time and resources are identified for the systematic development of IT capability both as a stand-alone element and as part of the teaching of other subjects.(Paragraphs 24, 42, 45, 49–51)

Standards of achievement

The GCSE and GCE results achieved nationally in information technology in 1994 are addressed in a section commencing at paragraph 69.

Key Stages 1 and 2

1 Work with IT is usually characterised by enthusiasm and lively, co-operative activities. Pupils support one another well and mostly have reasonable access to IT. In the best practice pupils are responsible for

looking after equipment and may acquire familiarity with input devices and major applications, such as word-processing and data handling. In well-structured situations pupils have opportunities for solving problems in data handling or control, and sometimes produce some original and productive ways of overcoming difficulties with the data or the peripherals used. The pupils involved then pick up much IT knowledge and skill.

2   At Key Stage 1 pupils are confident in the basic use of equipment and simple programs. Most are able to operate concept keyboards, (and by Year 2 QWERTY keyboards), load software, follow menus and print out their work.

3   At KS2 most pupils use keyboards confidently and, where available, mice, though their speed in locating keys is very variable. Almost all are able to use a word processor for writing and to amend spellings and punctuation. There is rather too much copy typing and little re-drafting. Many pupils are able to use graphics, occasionally also zooming facilities, and to position images at will around the screen. By the end of KS2 they are mostly able to set out title pages for their topic work, newspapers and other productions, using wordprocessor, graphics or desktop publishing (DTP) software. Many are able to search simple databases and produce related tables and graphs. Some work of outstanding quality has been seen at KS2, involving the imaginative use of computers and peripherals in datalogging and analysis in science and in mathematical problem solving.

4   The most disappointing feature at KS2, however, is the frequent lack of progress beyond KS1 levels of attainment. Although some data handling work of quality is seen, much work with databases is relatively unsophisticated, even where a school has access to CD-ROM. Graphical presentation of results is often mundane and lacking in commentary concerning meaning. Pupils are not confident with control, which is often absent after KS1.

5   Overall, in 71% of 120 KS1–2 lessons analysed, pupils attained average or better standards in IT in relation to their capability, compared with 77% for all subjects. In 20% of lessons IT attainment was good or very good in relation to pupils' capability, compared with 23% in other subjects overall.

6   Most pupils have not experienced all the relevant strands of IT capability by the time they leave primary school. Nevertheless some are able to learn new skills through their confidence with computers and various peripherals. The vast majority possess skills which are directly applicable to KS3 studies.

Key Stage 3

7   In relation to pupils' capabilities standards were satisfactory or better in 75% of lessons and good or very good in 23%. These are rather lower than the corresponding statistics for all subjects aggregated (81% and 31% respectively).

8   Overwhelmingly, IT elicits interest and enthusiasm from boys and girls, and they co-operate very readily and responsibly in its use. Attitudes to work with IT are generally very positive, and motivation to acquire relevant skills and to become autonomous users is generally high. What is most important to the quality of learning is the appropriateness of the stimuli and access offered to the individual pupil.

9   Typically, the range of applications in which pupils display competence at KS3 spans text handling, desktop publishing (DTP) including manipulation of text and graphics, and techniques of data storage and retrieval. In many schools KS3 pupils can apply totals and percentage calculations to straightforward tables of data in spreadsheets.

10   By the middle of the Key Stage boys and girls are generally confident and competent in operating equipment in lessons. Some achieve an enviable degree of fluency. Unfortunately, in most schools pupils have few opportunities to employ these skills and insights in the course of studying more than a couple of subjects at most.

11   Where IT is taught through one or more curriculum subjects, some fruitful and realistic contexts are provided for the application of IT. For instance, English lessons were used to introduce pupils to DTP software and they were charged with producing advertisements and articles about their chosen areas of interest, while other pupils were simultaneously investigating CD-ROM encyclopaedias in the library.

12   Such contexts can be very beneficial, and standards are high where pupils have been stimulated to operate at the highest technical and analytic levels of which they are individually capable, and have accessed appropriate sources and IT facilities at home or at school to produce useful outcomes.

13   Standards are low whenever pupils simply go through the motions of operating IT, eg manipulating images or retrieving from a pre-existing database on disk or CD-ROM, but without exercising much skill or judgement in presentation or analysis. There is evidence of much routine practice of low-level skills, eg the display of work in which only surface features of text or graphics are very competently and quickly altered, but where the impact of the message is not assessed sufficiently critically; sometimes such outcomes are not even saved on disk or paper.

Key Stage 4

14   In relation to capability, good or very good standards accounted for only about 25.5% of lessons (compared to 32% for all subjects). The percentage of lessons recording satisfactory or better achievement in terms of capability was 75%. This is about 7% below the corresponding figures for all other subjects.

15   There are clear indications that, in relation to capability, there are fewer good or very good standards being achieved in Year 10 than in Year 11. This may be due to differences between the years in terms of implementation of the National Curriculum: while more pupils in Year 10 have been observed doing work in IT as required by statute, those few in Year 11 who had elected for IT or computer studies registered more good or very good work (28.5%) compared with Year 10 (23.5%).

16   KS4 standards of the average pupil are approaching levels where they feel at home with generic wordprocessing and spreadsheet facilities available in the office and in post-16 education. Above all, most pupils have the confidence to learn new skills or refine those they already have in a particular application. The range of software applications available to a particular pupil remains variable, often depending on access outside lesson time. Coverage of the five strands of IT is

extremely patchy. Some fine work was observed in science and mathematics lessons with portable computers. These enabled pupils to work more flexibly on assignments involving measurement and exploratory data analysis both during and outside lesson time.

17   At this Key Stage many pupils are highly motivated by the technology as well as by any certification of IT which they work to gain. They perceive IT as providing a means of enhancing their coursework, and they acquire some additional skills and fluency in IT in the course of this work. Pupils' own time is used extensively in many areas of the school with IT facilities.

18   There is no evidence that user guides and manuals are used by pupils to develop autonomy in IT; most pupils prefer to ask a neighbour or the teacher to overcome their difficulties! There is much productive co-operation whenever there is IT-related work to be done, and much learning through sitting by the side of an expert.

Post-16

19   Too few IT and computing lessons were inspected post-16 to permit the writing of a meaningful section on standards.

Quality of teaching

Key Stages 1 and 2

20   The quality of teaching is satisfactory or better in only 71% of the 120 primary lessons seen compared with 75% for all subjects. Between 30% and 35% of lessons had good or very good teaching for IT, a comparable figure to lessons in all subjects.

21   Where standards of teaching are good, teachers have promoted IT through building its use into their schemes of work. Some programs used by pupils contribute to an aspect of the work in hand but also develop competence in basic IT. Teachers set appropriately challenging tasks with IT and arrange supervision of pupils' work. They themselves learn and apply new IT knowledge and skills, and develop pupils' IT capability by explicit teaching, thus encouraging pupils to become independent users of the technology. Pupils are taught to look after equipment and associated software. Non-teaching support, sometimes

by parents, is sensibly used to develop pupils' competence in IT, for example by promoting IT skills while wordprocessing a story.

22   Where teaching is unsatisfactory it is largely noted by its absence. Thus a teacher may just outline a task to pupils, suggest a piece of software, and let pupils get on with it. Occasionally, the teacher introduces a new item of software and then supervises individuals as they acquire familiarity with it. But generally pupils are not offered sufficient correction or advice if they execute tasks inefficiently or erroneously. For example, pupils may not be shown explicitly how to amend a piece of text at a particular location on the screen after positioning a cursor rather than deleting text already typed, or how to copy a section of text to another part of a document. Such lack of support results in some poor use of IT.

23   Teachers usually offer effective encouragement to pupils and respond helpfully to problems, where these become noticeable. This can be time-consuming, particularly where teachers lack expertise. Some very effective support from teachers and non-teaching assistants is noted, and some good choice of contexts for pupils to apply IT. Often, however, adults' expectations are low; there is little intervention in pupils' work to enhance challenge or to promote higher levels of IT capability; opportunities to develop an understanding of a concept may be missed, eg in control, through failure to reflect on pupils' experience of operating TV sets by remote controller.

Key Stages 3 and 4

24   At Key Stage 3, 73% of lessons have teaching which is satisfactory or better, with 34% being good or very good. These figures are 7% below the corresponding ones for all subjects when aggregated. At Key Stage 4 standards of teaching are close to those for all subjects, at around 80% satisfactory or better and 41% good or very good. The latter figures may reflect the fact that more lessons seen in Key Stage 4 were taught by IT specialist teachers to GCSE examination groups.

25   IT lessons at these Key Stages are mostly practical and take place in computer rooms. Typically, a teacher sets the class a task after a brief introduction, and circulates, perhaps with the help of another teacher, to provide individual help. If IT is taught through another subject, eg

technology, a task might be to use DTP facilities to design an advertisement for placement in a local newspaper to sell a garden design business. In science a bubble potometer model might be used to examine factors that change the rate of transpiration. In an IT lesson 1pupils might interrogate a database about birds in the British Isles. Teacher/pupil relations are usually friendly and relaxed.

26   Where teaching is good the work has been well planned and set in a sensible context; command of the subject by teaching or support staff is adequate, even lessons in which pupils are working individually start on time, pupils are clear about the tasks being demanded of them, there is adequate differentiation of activities where necessary, and pupils have opportunities to display initiative in designing or in solving problems and to work collaboratively. Expectations of outcomes are high.

27   The quality of teaching is unsatisfactory where teaching is over-directed and unrelated to pupils' previous attainments in IT and their interests; teachers' command of the subject is poor; course materials and computer resources are poorly organised; the teaching is interrupted because of technical problems either in the computer room or beyond it; and the teachers' expectations are low, eg when the teacher saves a pupil's work in Autosketch without attempting to teach the pupil how to save it for herself in future.

28   At KS4 there is some fine teaching and close questioning of pupils on such topics as survey construction, privacy and the security of computer-based data. The latter topics form part of PoS devoted to the effects of IT applications on the individual and society, and rarely get a mention in the evidence except in the context of work targeted on GCSE in IT or computer studies. Specialist work is frequently of good standard, with more good or very good teaching in Year 11 than Year 10.

29   Where learning is good it is associated with some differentiation of tasks, particularly after the initial few lessons of introduction to a school's computer facilities or a new software package, and with a purposeful development of knowledge and skills which takes account of where the pupil starts. Within such planned provision pupils have opportunities and stimuli to exercise choice and display initiative. It is,

however, rare at Key Stage 3 for homework or sustained project work to be set for IT, except where IT is taught as part of another subject.

30   The quality of learning IT through applications within the curriculum during these Key Stages varies in different subjects. Learning and use of IT skills is most effective when subject departments devote time to teaching the skills themselves or plan to delay their use of IT until pupils have acquired the necessary skills elsewhere. Some valuable computer applications in subjects appear, however, to require, and to reinforce, only modest levels of IT capability.

31   Learning is poor where pupils are directed to engage in narrowly focused exercises in IT, which fail to kindle interest or to lead to challenging outcomes; tasks are set which are fairly trivial, or too open-ended and ill-defined at too early a stage. Sometimes the learning environment is uncomfortable, or lacking in space for working at and away from equipment.

Post-16

32   Too few IT and computing lessons were inspected post-16 to permit the writing of a meaningful section on teaching.

Assessment, recording and reporting

33   There is a great variety of practice in the assessment of pupils' IT capability. It is common for schools to record the topics covered or applications encountered in the course of the Key Stage. At KS1 and 2 there is widespread use of Statement of Attainment (SoA) tick lists based on teachers' retrospective views of pupils' performance. The recording, let alone reporting, thus does not always reflect actual achievement in terms of NC levels in IT capability. The results of some painstaking assessment at the end of KS1 were rarely used to inform subsequent teaching of IT capability.

34   At KS3 and 4 recording of pupils' experiences with IT is also more common than recording and reporting of actual achievements. Pupils may complete self-assessments as part of their records of achievement, and these provide further insights into experiences gained and sometimes levels of competence, but not necessarily in NC terms. Where IT

is reported, it is usually in terms of attitudes or coverage rather than capability.

35   There is hardly any monitoring of the standards of teachers' assessment at KS 3 and 4 to ensure consistency of judgement amongst staff within schools who are involved in assessing IT. By and large schools do not conform to the requirements of NC assessment and reporting of IT.

Curriculum content

36   At KS1–2 in most schools IT is being marginalised, especially at KS2, by the need to cover other aspects of the NC. Most schools have policies concerning the use of IT, and resources are available to give effect to them. But IT capability is not generally developed with rigour after KS1. A majority of teachers refer to IT in their planning, but this is usually a brief reference to the programs to be used rather than to the skills to be developed.

37   In Year 2 an average of about 6% of the curriculum is spent by pupils on technology, which includes both design and technology (DT) and the main application of IT by pupils. This rises to an average of 6.7% in Year 6. The use of IT is frequently integrated into literacy, numeracy or topic work, but there is little assurance that every pupil receives the entitlement specified in the PoS.

38   In only a minority of schools do schemes of work for classes show that all strands have been planned for. Work observed shows that pupils have experienced the various strands, although their specific attainments are rarely monitored and recorded, except at the end of KS1.

39   Much of the work at both Key Stages relates to the communication of information, though most schools include some data handling. The introduction to control technology is spasmodic and very few schools touch on the applications and effects of IT. At Key Stage 1 there is a disappointingly high use of programs providing drill and practice, which adds little to pupils' IT capability.

40   At KS 3–4 most schools offer specific teaching of IT skills as modules within technology, personal and social education (PSE) or combined studies; as a separate course; or as an integral part of the curriculum of various subjects. Pupils are likely to encounter a combination of these approaches as they move through the Key Stages. Most schools possess policy statements on IT and its delivery. These are often agreed with those subject departments which contribute to the development of IT capability. Co-operative arrangements for developing IT capability work well in schools where they are monitored by senior management.

41   Where there is little or no timetabled provision for teaching IT at KS3, responsibility for developing IT rests almost entirely with different departments. Such arrangements mostly do not work well. Often there is a mismatch between agreed policies to develop IT through work in departments, and the way these actually operate. For instance:

- schemes of work in contributing subjects do not always reflect the policies;

- such schemes are not explicit enough concerning the levels of attainment in IT which will be promoted in each subject;

- teachers in contributing departments are reluctant to be involved in assessing pupils' IT attainments;

- the applications chosen reinforce mainly the lower levels of IT capability, not higher attainment levels;

- the skills, knowledge and understanding of IT developed through cross-curricular teaching do not span the entire PoS for IT capability.

Most pupils in such schools are, therefore, not getting their NC entitlement in IT; the PoS in IT are not reaching the majority of the pupils.

42   Where IT is taught at some stage as a separate module or stand-alone course, coverage is more rigorous, but there are not always sufficient opportunities to ensure that acquired IT skills are applied to work in other subjects. Although standards of attainment in IT are often higher where there are timetabled IT courses, some of the work taught

in such courses or modules is undemanding, unrelated to pupils' interests and previous experiences of IT, and unrelated to pupils' other studies. For the majority of pupils good standards of attainment and learning follow mixed arrangements: where some timetabled teaching of IT at KS3 is combined with well-supported opportunities to apply skills in other subjects.

Resources and their management

Staffing

43   In KS1–2 teachers are now familiar with many items of software and growing in confidence with IT, though few are abreast of IT capability as defined in the National Curriculum. The quality of IT work tends to depend on the attitudes towards IT of individual teachers, the importance which they attach to developing pupils' IT capability, and the level of support available in school from the headteacher and IT co-ordinator. Where the latter is responsible for more than just the physical resources and software, and has adequate time to provide support to colleagues, more staff are able to sustain work of quality which is appropriate for pupils as they move up the school.

44   In both primary and secondary Key Stages the majority of teachers are not qualified to teach more than a limited range of the PoS for IT. Their command of IT is generally poor compared with other subjects. At KS3 there is enthusiasm, and some readiness to be involved in delivering aspects of IT capability. There is some good team teaching in an attempt to share skills or to ensure that IT capability is addressed, and technical problems are overcome, when IT is taught in the context of a subject. Often teachers' lack of confidence with increasingly varied, or newly acquired, computer facilities inhibits teaching or assessment of IT capability. Some good use of technicians and other ancillary help is reported, and has overcome lack of teacher confidence and problems of classroom management. There is much evidence that in-service training in IT which teachers receive is now largely provided in-house; little of schools' devolved budgets is spent on purchasing IT training expertise from outside. But there remains a massive need for the continued training of staff who are occasional users, teachers and assessors of IT, as well as those who offer them IT leadership.

45   Effective co-ordination of the work of several different staff proves challenging for many schools. Where co-ordination is successful, IT co-ordinators have a suitable role and structure defined, and have the necessary qualifications, personal skills and seniority to form links with, and work alongside, colleagues. Many schools are critically dependent on too few staff to implement their curricular policies in IT and maintain the schools' IT facilities.

Resources for learning and accommodation

46   At KS1–2 there is mostly adequate provision of equipment, though some of it is ageing and there are instances of only limited ranges of suitable software being available. Few schools now have fewer than one microcomputer per class, and many have more. A large majority of schools now have at least one microcomputer per class, and many have more. Ratios of 1 computer to 17 pupils or better are not uncommon. Some facilities are extremely effectively used, others remain idle or are used mainly to limited effect, eg to provide drill exercises, or to present information attractively rather than to help in its compilation, sensible storage or analysis.

47   The supply of library texts and other sources of information about computers and their applications, such as communications and control, is generally poor.

48   The sample of primary schools inspected was too small to yield meaningful statistics on the availability of hardware. In 701 secondary schools the average microcomputer-to-pupil ratio was around one to eleven. The distribution was as follows:

Pupils to one micro	4–6	7–9	10–12	13–15	16–18	19–21	22–24	25+
Percentage of schools	7	28	33	19	9	2	0	1

49   In the majority of KS3–4 lessons, resources issues are not limiting the work; indeed, IT based facilities are more frequently considered to contribute positively to the lesson. Positive factors noted are the appropriate number of computers for a class; availability of work for pupils not engaged in working at computers; and a variety of useful software

packages and databases. Negative factors include crowding around too few computer screens; printers not being located near the class; network or peripheral breakdowns; and worksheets and courseware providing too little challenge or no opportunity to undertake extensive independent study. Books on IT and guides for users of software are few and far between and hardly used.

50   It is certainly the case that, where pupils are heavily exposed to IT, standards of attainment in IT capability are higher. But exposure to IT is as much a function of the availability of physical resources as of the management and organisation of the curriculum, the provision of support and the monitoring by senior management of how well IT capability is being delivered through the school's chosen mechanism. By itself, a favourable pupil-to-microcomputer ratio does not necessarily assure consistently high-quality work with IT though it does indicate that the school management is prepared to invest and to develop this aspect of the curriculum.

51   The application of IT in various areas of the curriculum is often dependent on the availability and location of IT facilities, or the timetabling of their use. Most primary classrooms now have a computer, either static or mobile, and sometimes the documents relating to the available software are also accessible. Where IT capability is being taught in secondary schools, computer rooms or areas in which computers are clustered together in departments are invariably used, and their design and appointment most often draw favourable comment. Occasionally, overcrowding prevents teachers from supervising pupils' work properly and involves too many pupils working at one screen; this reduces effective lesson time for individuals, and the likelihood that practical work will be productive for many pupils.

Inspection issues

Inspection development

52 Inspections carried out under Section 9 of the Education (Schools) Act 1992 began in September 1993. Inspection teams have made a good start in meeting the requirements of the Framework for the Inspection of Schools; they have become more confident as the year has progressed and early uncertainties have been resolved in many cases. This part of the subject profile draws together some of the key issues for further improving the quality and standard of inspection. Many issues are similar from one subject to another; where there are subject-specific matters these are indicated.

53 Some examples of inspection writing are included. They are not intended to be viewed as models or templates but illustrate how inspectors have effectively completed forms and met Framework requirements.

Evidence gathering

54 Inspectors generally sample a good range of IT work of different year groups, abilities and key stages across the compulsory years of education. The inspection of IT has for some inspectors not been straightforward. IT is an aspect of the NC which may be taught either through specific lessons or through application in other subjects. The time available to inspectors for inspecting IT varies considerably in different schools, and needs to permit the assessment of all aspects of IT capability, especially where its delivery is through several curriculum subjects. It is important that, where a school has a sixth form, post-16 work is fairly represented in the sampling. Inspectors use evidence from a good range of sources but discussion with pupils could be used more often to provide evidence of precise levels of attainment in IT. This is particularly important where only a few IT lessons are available for inspection. It is also important that clear reference is made to the source of evidence when reaching judgements. The Supplementary Evidence Form provides a means of documenting evidence and judgements from sources other than lessons and could be more widely used.

Lesson Observation Forms

55   The majority of Lesson Observation Forms are completed conscientiously, with attention to the relevant evaluation criteria. Inspectors could usefully check that comments reflect the character and detail of the subject and that all fields on the form are correctly coded; in particular that, where grades for achievement relate to IT capability, irrespective of the subject in which the work in IT was seen.

56   In relation to the **content** of lessons, the majority of inspectors adequately indicate the topic of lessons usually with reference to the National Curriculum Order. Further details of the lesson activities would be helpful in setting the context. An example of a 'Content' section follows.

Years 3/4 (Class topic is "Houses")

Pupils had already used IT to graph the types of houses they lived in, and had neatly produced estate-agent type brochures of their own homes. They were entering the details about their houses into a prepared database. This was intended to cover Te5 Level 2.

57   Inspectors draw on their professional knowledge and experience to make overall judgements about the **achievements** of pupils. Responding to the Framework requirements to assess pupils' achievements in relation to national norms and taking account of pupils' abilities has not proved easy. Revised requirements and guidance published in June 1994 should help inspectors in making these distinct judgements. To support judgements it is important that inspectors clearly identify and record what pupils know, understand and can do and set achievements in the context of National Curriculum Statements of Attainment. An example of an 'Achievement' section from Lesson Observation Forms follows.

Years 3/4, mixed ability

Achievement (age referenced): Brochures were neat and resembled a commercial format. Text entry to the computer under specific data headings was slow. Pupils did not recognise that space was restricted and that abbreviations would be necessary, but were able to talk about the problems that might arise from incorrect data entry. They recognised the advantages of using IT databases and knew what the database would ultimately provide. Te5 Level 3-4. Grade 3

58   Clear evidence of pupils' attitudes to learning and their behaviour in lessons is usually given, and this is reflected in the grade given for **quality of learning**. Greater prominence should be given to other attributes of learning, particularly pupils' progress in lessons and the particular features of learning in information technology included in section 6.5(ii) of Part 4 of the *Handbook for the Inspection of schools*. An example follows.

Year 13 AS-Level

Pupils work individually with little interaction to produce a database to hold information. Their confidence in the use of the (advanced) features of the database software helps them to progress quickly. They engage in useful problem-solving to determine the record and field structures, but their plans for checking test data are not rigorous. Students are really well motivated but not organised to brainstorm ideas for practical activities. Little evidence of wider reading about IT. Grade 3

59   Inspectors usually cite relevant evidence when judging the **quality of teaching**, and evaluation is based on the criteria in the Framework. They need to check that the full range of criteria is used, including teachers' command of the subject. In the following example, a number of attributes of teaching are referred to.

Year 9

Some teaching of whole group around computers – teacher and pupils demonstrating; visibility of screen not good for everybody. Teacher does not check that everybody has understood, and assumes that their listening implies understanding and retention. Most of the period is then spent by pupils working in pairs at their micros with teacher walking around to support. When a problem arises concerning totalling, the whole group is brought together again for another demonstration and the majority of the class has to re-enter their data as numbers (with no unit names) – much time wasted. There is no planning on paper. No differentiation. No reference materials for pupils to use; teacher has fair knowledge of subject, but pupils started task with insufficient information. Grade 4

60   The Lesson Observation Form could be more widely used to indicate contributions made by IT-related activities to key skills, such as literacy and numeracy, and to learning in other areas of the curriculum, whatever the observed learning of IT capability. The Form also provides the opportunity to signal the impact of contributory factors, such as staff expertise, in-service training or hardware provision on achievements and the quality of learning. This evidence can be drawn on when compiling the Subject Evidence Form.

Subject Evidence Forms

61   Subject Evidence Forms are usually fully completed, very often thoroughly and thoughtfully. In most cases, a wide range of evidence appears to have been used. Inspectors need to check that reference to this range of evidence is sufficiently explicit in the relevant sections of the form and to ensure that the emphasis is towards evaluation rather than description.

62   Particular attention is given to aspects of standards of achievement and the quality of learning and teaching although, as in Lesson Observation Forms, in considering the quality of learning more emphasis is placed on pupils' attitudes and behaviour than on their skills as learners. When commenting on examination results as part of their evaluation of standards of achievement, inspectors should ensure that the evidence includes the basis for any comparisons with national data.

63   Completed sections, from separate schools, on standards of achievement and the quality of learning and teaching from Subject Evidence Forms follow. They provide adequate evidence on which to base the subject paragraph for the report.

Standards of Achievement

Standards of achievement were in line with national expectations in about half the lessons seen, with marked variation between classes taught by different teachers. Generally the younger pupils achieved at appropriate levels for their abilities but there was insufficient development of their skills in later years. For example, Year 7 pupils were able to edit and format text (Te5, level 3) quite competently. Year 8 and 9 pupils were beginning to adjust page layouts and write for specific audiences (working towards levels 4/5), but used cumbersome techniques and were unsure of more complex format-ting. At Key Stage 4, there was very little progression in IT skills for those taking the minimum entitlement course. Year 10 pupils' achievement in the other IT strands prescribed by the National Curriculum was minimal – where pupils tried to set up a database, they struggled with outdated software that required an unrealistic memory of computer syntax. In Year 11, pupils discussed wider applications of IT in society, but for a group taking GCSE Computer Studies needed more sophisticated knowledge of the underlying principles. GCSE results in 1992 (there was no CS option in 1992) were low: only 7% A–C grades.

Quality of Learning

Pupils in Key Stages 1 and 2 learn a wide range of IT applications, particularly in data handling and communication, but less so in measurement and control. Much of the work done supports learn-ing in various subjects, and pupils enjoy using computers in class-room and extra-curricular activities. Opportunities for extended work with IT vary from class to class. Those pupils seen using IT showed competence and confidence within the tasks set, but few showed the versatility to develop beyond them; to cope with a range of problems without support and to acquire wider knowledge, understanding and skills.

Quality of Teaching

The quality of teaching was satisfactory or better in 75% of lessons, and at Key Stage 3 it was good in 40% of lessons. The lessons had definite aims which were clearly communicated to the pupils. Teachers intervened at appropriate stages in the work to give praise and encouragement. When needed the staff also gave necessary help to particular pupils. In some lessons staff with particular IT experi-ence donated their "preparation" periods to give assistance to colleagues using computers. The use of IT was integrated into lessons with varying degrees of coherence, and there was little evidence of the planned progression of IT skills. There was some evidence of staff unfamiliarity with the full range of features of the software used.

64   When considering features such as the resources for learning, management and the quality of teaching, the emphasis should be on the evaluation of the effects these have on the standards achieved and the quality of learning. The following extracts from the 'Contributory factors' sections of the Subject Evidence Form include clear judgements about features of provision and some indications of their effects.

Teaching and Support Staff

Many IT skills are taught by teachers who are not IT specialists; this adds strength to the meaningful contexts for IT activities, but leaves some weaknesses in the levels of IT capability being developed. Much progress has been made in ensuring that teachers are developing their own capabilities, although there is still a great deal of continuing INSET required for all teachers involved. The support which teachers and pupils get from the IT technician in the resources centre is of a very high quality, and is invaluable to them. Such support would also have been very valuable in the context of the wider school uses of IT. No specific time is currently allocated for the IT technician to manage the network. This has meant that maintenance and avoidable system failures have sometimes prevented the IT co-ordinator from devoting sufficient time to his responsibilities for pupil assessment in IT.

Curriculum Content

In Key Stage 3, the school had identified the first subjects to be linked with IT – English, mathematics, science and the humanities – supported by one period of IT per week. An outline programme of work each term had been drawn up, with each unit being planned in more detail a half-term at a time. The level of expectation in these outline programmes was quite high, but the levels of skill required had not been fully analysed and understood by all members of the departments concerned. The actual linking was not yet fully in place. For example, in Year 7, a stand-alone unit of IT skills was being taught, with pupils having few opportunities to practise them; in Year 8, IT was not synchronised with history, so pupils came to the IT lessons without having the necessary knowledge, for example, of the dissolution of the monasteries. Year 9 were writing for a teenage audience, but this work was being done too late as it linked with English work done the previous term.

Judgement Recording Statements

65 The Judgement Recording Statements are usually fully completed. Inspectors need to ensure that all available evidence is considered in arriving at judgements for inclusion in the proforma. The purpose and use of Judgement Recording Statements are outlined in Appendix C of Part 3 of the *Handbook for the Inspection of Schools.*

Subject sections in inspection reports

66 Most IT subject sections in inspection reports meet the Framework requirements and those seen well matched the evidence in the Subject Evidence Forms. They give appropriate emphasis to standards of achievement and the quality of learning and teaching, and are based on current provision, rather than schools' hopes for the future. Inspectors need to ensure that overall judgements are clear and succinct and draw on all the evidence available, and that factors which impact on standards of achievement and quality of learning are clearly identified.

67 The following extracts from four reports illustrate writing about standards of achievement, quality of learning and teaching and a contributory factor. The characteristics of IT are evident.

School A

In Key Stages 3 and 4 pupils' standards of achievement are generally at a level commensurate with their age and ability: selecting appropriate software packages and using spreadsheets, databases, WP, DTP and art packages effectively. Achievement within the monitoring and control strand is good in Key Stage 4. Oral skills are good and pupils described their practical work with ability and enthusiasm. The work was contextualised within the curriculum subjects which pupils were studying but too much work is still drafted by hand with pupils being required to produce "fair copy" using the computers and printers. Pupils are competent and confident in the use of IT to generate graphs....

School B

....The pupils have a potentially rich environment in which to develop their learning in IT, but in some lessons in both Key Stage 3 & 4 all the pupils were working at the same pace with little opportunity to display initiative, work in groups or develop a real understanding of IT. In many lessons the classroom layout and its use made group work difficult. Discussion of IT issues was more frequent where IT was an element in another subject. Post-16 students were encouraged to use IT both inside and outside lessons to extend their presentational skills in various subjects. In all age ranges the pupils were disciplined and on-task in IT lessons, although some inactivity was observed whilst pupils waited to receive attention from the teacher. Insufficient materials, such as prompt cards, were available for individual study and reference....

School C

....Teaching was good in some classes, weaker in others. Lessons were planned with broad learning aims in mind but the specific skills to be learnt were not always fully articulated. There was little systematic planned input or whole class teaching in some classes. Most pupils were given the same problems or tasks, with the more able expected to progress further and to learn more advanced IT facilities and techniques. This worked well at times, but in practice there was not always a match of challenge and progress to ability and pupils' previous IT experience. Pupils' work was marked regularly, with technical errors pointed out. Comments did not always help pupils to develop the content or improve the techniques used.

School D

....The school's cross-curriculum working party has undertaken useful work developing a whole school policy for IT. Its work has led to some progression in the development of IT capability across the curriculum. Some departments have introduced IT to support their work; others have taken little action. Limited strategies exist to ensure consistency in implementation. Pupils' experience of IT *capability is, therefore, generally limited to Communication and Handling of Information. In a few lessons work is undertaken on the Application and Effects strand. Modelling is developed by the use of spreadsheets, Logo programming and simulations. The Measurement and Control strand received no attention. The school is clearly not meeting the requirements of the National Curriculum in IT, and needs to clarify the roles, responsibilities and inter-relationship between heads of department and the school's co-ordinator for IT.*

School E

....The level of IT resources in the school is good, and effective use is made of equipment in the BIT area. The network offers pupils extensive learning opportunities and is efficiently used by them. Its operating performance, however, has been variable and needs to be improved. Networked machines located in some departments have not always been used; this is because there has not been sufficient INSET for staff or because departmental staff regard other machines and software as more appropriate for their subject. Although the pupil:computer ratio of about 9:1 compares favourably with the LEA average, many of the non-networked machines are older models, which will not run modern, easy-to-use integrated software; this constrains the teaching and learning.

68   In writing to the Framework requirements, inspectors need to check that a comment is included on compliance with statutory requirements and that key issues for action in the subject are clearly given. These are helpful to schools in their action planning.

The interpretation of subject performance data

GCSE Computer Studies 1994

69   No Computer Studies examination with published results in 1994 corresponded to all five strands of IT capability and caution therefore needs to be exercised in relating any examination statistics to performance in IT as defined in the National Curriculum. The term Computer Studies is used here to cover all the syllabuses which

conform with the GCSE National Criteria for Computer Studies, which, in 1993 and 1994, include the titles Information Technology and Information Systems.

70   The performance of the pupils in maintained schools who took GCSE Computer Studies (10.6% of the cohort of 15-year-olds in 1994) matched closely the overall profile for all GCSE subjects. This general match in performance, however, concealed substantial variations between schools whose policies towards entry for Computer Studies ranged from encouragement for a small group of able pupils to gain an additional qualification to a view that Computer Studies can offer useful stimuli to those who are attracted to practical work and whose lack of ability or motivation leads them away from the more traditional subjects.

71   The popularity of Computer Studies as an examination subject has been declining over recent years. This is largely because schools have been concentrating IT resources and expertise on support for work throughout the curriculum rather than on specialist courses. Business education, in particular, has increasingly featured the use of IT and has attracted many of those who might formerly have opted for Computer Studies.

72   Another trend has been the increasing bias towards boys in the entry pattern, from a boy-to-girl split of 59%:41% in 1992 to 64%:36% in 1993 and 1994. In spite of this skewed entry pattern the performance of boys and girls as separate groups matched their performances across all subjects, the girls generally being more successful.

73   The proportion of the cohort taking Computer Studies varied little between comprehensive, grammar and modern schools. The only notable feature of performance related to type of school is that the grammar school entry for computer studies traditionally performed somewhat less well compared with its performance in all other subjects. Thus, in 1993, 74.4% of computer studies entries from grammar schools were graded A to C, compared with 89.5% in aggregate for all other subjects. In 1994 the difference was smaller: 82% were graded A* to C in computer studies compared with 89.5% in all other subjects; and 12.7% of the grammar school entry obtained an A* grade.

74   Failure to complete the examination requirements, leading to an X result, was 3.7% for computer studies compared with 3% for all other subjects aggregated. One reason for an X grade may be the heavy coursework requirement, which leads to assignments remaining unfinished or being completed too late.

AS and A-level Computing 1994

75   Of those pupils in maintained schools entered for at least one A or AS level subject, only 2.7% took Computing at A-level and 0.8% at AS level. There has been significant growth in entry for the subject in recent years but most of this growth has been concentrated outside schools, where group sizes are usually larger and appropriate software, hardware and staffing more plentiful.

76   The entry from maintained schools was very strongly biased towards boys, who outnumbered girls by almost five to one in A-level computing and by three to one in AS. Also of note was that the girls, for whom results across all subjects were only marginally lower than for the boys, performed substantially less well in Computing, particularly at A- level where the mean difference was more than half a grade.

77   The results in Computing at A-level were generally less good than the pattern for all subjects, down by about quarter of a grade on average.

Update on developments in Information Technology

The review of the National Curriculum and associated issues

78   The new Orders for Technology now clearly separate the Information Technology component from Design and Technology for most purposes, including pupil assessment. The new Order has not drastically changed expectations of what pupils should be able to do with IT, except in some details, eg that "pre-modelling" experiences are now added to the Key Stage 1 Programme of Study; measurement has been taken out of the Key Stage 2; and the various conceptual strands of the old Order are now grouped as two interrelated themes across the four

key stages. Standards of achievement should be judged from September 1995 in terms of the new Level Descriptions.

79   The Order in every subject except PE indicates that work in that subject should involve applications of IT where appropriate. The appropriateness of applications in terms of their relevance to studying particular subjects has been consulted on and debated nationally. Some non-Statutory Guidance has recently been published by SCAA containing suggestions of appropriate IT applications in each subject, and indicating that more relevant materials will be available from the National Council for Educational Technology.

80   In judging whether a school is complying with the NC Orders it will therefore be necessary to ascertain not only whether the school is offering the PoS which are to result in IT capability as described in the Order for IT, but whether it offers opportunities in various subjects to apply, practise and develop such capability. For pupils starting Key Stage 4, however, the Secretary of State has relaxed for two years the requirement to study the new PoS for technology. This means that pupils starting Key Stage 4 in September 1995 will not now be required to develop their IT capability beyond Year 9.

81   Pupils who are presently in Year 11 do have to continue studying IT but there is no requirement for them to be assessed in it. It is therefore likely that some pupils who started examination courses in IT or information systems when they were in Year 10 will have abandoned them in favour of other types of IT provision, or that courses originally designated as leading to external examinations may have been redesignated as non-examination courses in Year 11.

CD-ROM in primary schools

82   Well over 20% of primary schools now have at least one CD-ROM system with a range of software for use by pupils. By September 1995 the number of primary schools with CD-ROMs may have nearly doubled following the further injection of DFE funds in February-March 1995. Training for teachers in the use of the systems was arranged by the suppliers of the systems or their agents. There was little provision for training in the classroom use of specific items of software.

83   These systems may in some cases have added significantly to a school's ability to be enterprising in handling aspects of IT capability. The quality of use of the systems and software may be an issue for the schools concerned. Inspectors may wish to comment on whether and how these new facilities are helping pupils to engage in serious information handling and other creative work and enhancing their IT capability. Care may be needed in ascertaining appropriateness of use; whether pupils are aware of the accuracy, and reliability of the information they handle; and whether they become judicious in the use of these powerful media.

Support for IT in schools

84   The Grants for Education Support and Training (GEST) used to have a separate category for IT which did not have to be devolved to schools. This is not to be so during 1995-96. From April 1995 GEST will not have a separate category for IT. The funds for IT have been consolidated in a larger category – School Effectiveness. All but 20% of this category of GEST funding has to be devolved to schools in accordance with a formula laid down by DFE.

85   Schools will therefore be receiving their share of the School Effectiveness GEST from April 1995. If past experience is a guide, more in-service training will be undertaken by in-house experts or by contracted external agencies, such as LEA IT centres, private consultants and HE providers. The availability of credible, well-informed technical and professional support for IT from within or outside the school, and the appropriateness of the in-service training provided to the school may be an issue for inspectors to take account of, and if necessary explore.

GNVQ developments

86   The first GNVQs are already running in many school sixth forms. In line with government policy increased participation is expected in both sixth forms and at KS4, covering GNVQ levels 1, 2 and 3 – Foundation, Intermediate and Advanced. There are two aspects which relate directly to IT – the IT Core Skills units, which must be completed at the relevant level for the award of any GNVQ, and the GNVQ in IT.

87   The IT Core Skills Units cover four elements: preparing information; processing information; presenting information; and evaluating the use of IT. There are links with National Curriculum IT capability, though the emphasis is more strongly towards the strands of communicating and handling information than modelling, control and measurement. The style of the requirements is also more prescriptive and relates more closely to standard business and industry practices. The differences of approach to IT between NC and GNVQ, and in particular the means of gathering evidence about achievement, are substantial.

88   Progression between the levels in the IT Core Skills units is broadly similar to progression through National Curriculum IT capability, depending on increasing breadth in using IT applications and increasing complexity in the operations performed. There is an intended link between the levels, subject to the significant qualifications mentioned in the previous paragraph: level 1 Core Skills units relate to National Curriculum levels 4 and below; level 2 Core Skills units relate to NC levels 5 and 6; level 3 Core Skills units relate to NC level 7. Future development of the NCVQ Core Skills units at levels 4 and 5 are intended to relate respectively to NC levels 8 and beyond.

89   The GNVQ in IT is being piloted at Foundation, Intermediate and Advanced levels in a limited number of centres. In common with other GNVQs, it requires candidates to complete a number of mandatory units at the appropriate level (3, 4 and 8 respectively for Foundation, Intermediate and Advanced levels), a number of optional units (3, 2 and 4 respectively) and each of the three Core Skills units: Communication; Application of Number; IT. The Foundation award is deemed to show a level of achievement similar to four GCSEs at grades D to F, Intermediate to be of comparable standard and coverage to four or five GCSEs at grade C and above, and Advanced to be a standard equivalent to two A levels supplemented by the Core Skills units.

90   A GCSE or A/AS level syllabus is normally studied through a course of a set duration designed for the purpose. Partial accreditation is not usually available. The situation is rather different for GNVQs, where students may complete and receive accreditation for units, individually or in combination, over a period of years. Failure to meet all the requirements of a unit carries no lasting penalty as the unit may be

taken again when the student is ready. It is normal for students to expect to accumulate units to a full GNVQ, and to plan to do so over a set period of time, but variations are accommodated. The Part One GNVQs at Foundation and Intermediate levels, intended for, and being piloted with some Key Stage 4 pupils share the same characteristics, but with an expectation that pupils will complete the whole qualification within two years. IT is not one of the Part One GNVQs being piloted from September 1995 but is expected to feature in the second pilot phase a year later.

91   The requirements of the units of the GNVQ in IT incorporate much of the detail of National Curriculum IT capability, and at Intermediate and Advanced levels much of the content of IT syllabuses and some elements of A-level Computing, but the emphasis is different. Skills and knowledge are specified in considerable detail rather than being left largely implicit in the application of IT. In addition the practices, roles and responsibilities of IT staff and the IT industry feature strongly.

Annex

GCSE results for 15 year olds[1] for Computer Studies 1994

Type of School		Number of 15 year old pupils entered	1994									Average points score[3]	% A*-C grades	% A*-G grades	1993		1992[2]	
			Percentages achieving grades												Average points score[3]	% A-C grades	Average points score[3]	% A-C grades
			A*	A	B	C	D	E	F	G	U							
Comprehensive		37824	3.3	8.0	14.2	21.7	15.4	16.2	10.2	5.7	1.4	4.35	47.1	94.6	3.97	45.2	4.06	46.3
Selective		1243	12.7	19.3	28.5	21.5	8.8	5.4	1.9	0.7	0.0	5.78	82.0	98.8	5.28	74.0	5.39	77.2
Modern		1200	1.3	3.0	11.9	22.3	18.5	22.6	10.8	6.3	1.7	3.97	38.5	96.7	3.49	31.4	3.80	42.7
Maintained	All pupils	40267	3.5	8.2	14.5	21.7	15.3	16.1	9.9	5.6	1.4	4.39	47.9	94.8	4.01	45.8	4.09	47.0
	Boys	25597	3.1	7.4	14.1	20.7	15.4	16.5	10.7	6.4	1.6	4.28	45.3	94.3	3.87	43.0	3.93	43.3
	Girls	14670	4.2	9.4	15.3	23.4	15.1	15.3	8.6	4.2	1.0	4.57	52.5	95.7	4.25	50.9	4.30	52.3
All Subjects Maintained	All pupils		2.1	8.4	16.4	20.5	18.9	14.5	10.2	4.5	1.5	4.40	47.4	95.5	4.12	46.3	4.14	45.0

1 Aged 15 on 31/8/93
2 1992 results include a small amount of data from special schools
3 Calculated on basis A*=8, A=7, B=6, C=5, D=4, E=3, F=2, G=1

– less than 100 candidates
* more than 100 and less than 500 candidates
x information not available

GCE AS results for Computer Studies 1994

Type of School		Number of candidates	Percentages achieving grades							% A–B grades	% A–E grades	Average points score[p]	1993 % A–B grades	1993 % A–E grades	1992 % A–B grades	1992 % A–E grades
			A	B	C	D	E	N	U							
Maintained	All pupils	906	8.4	10.9	18.8	20.2	19.0	14.1	6.5	19.3	77.3	2.0	17.2	71.8	16.0	70.8
	Boys	685	9.2	11.8	18.2	19.6	18.7	14.5	6.0	21.0	77.5	2.1	18.4	72.0	15.9	71.6
	Girls	221	5.9	8.1	20.4	22.2	19.9	13.1	8.1	14.0	76.5	1.9	12.8	71.1	16.4	68.3
All subjects																
Maintained	All pupils		7.1	10.2	14.8	17.9	18.2	12.9	15.1	17.3	68.2	1.8	17.0	65.5	16.6	65.4

− less than 100 candidates

* more than 100 and less than 500 candidates

p Calculated on basis A=5, B=4, C=3, D=2, E=1

The number of pupils taking AS levels is insufficient to yield a meaningful analysis by type of maintained school

GCE A-Level results for Computer Studies 1994

Type of School		Number of candidates	1994										1993		1992	
			Percentages achieving grades							% A-B grades	% A-E grades		% A-B grades	% A-E grades	% A-B grades	% A-E grades
			A	B	C	D	E	N	U							
Comprehensive		2441	8.8	11.3	15.8	19.2	17.7	13.7	12.1	20.1	72.7		19.9	73.2	16.4	75.7
Selective		366	21.3	16.1	18.3	16.4	11.7	10.7	3.8	37.4	83.9		36.5	91.4	34.8	92.0
Modern		24	–	–	–	–	–	–	–	–	–		–	–	13.2	73.6
Maintained	All pupils*	2831	10.4	11.9	16.0	18.8	17.1	13.2	11.1	22.3	74.1		21.9	75.5	18.4	77.5
	Boys	2380	11.2	13.2	16.3	18.3	16.6	12.6	10.3	24.4	75.6		23.7	77.2	20.0	78.3
	Girls	451	6.0	5.5	14.0	21.5	19.3	16.4	15.1	11.5	66.3		13.0	67.2	11.0	73.8
All subjects Maintained	All pupils		13.1	16.2	18.5	18.9	15.2	9.4	7.5	29.3	81.9		28.0	79.7	26.4	78.6

– less than 100 candidates

* more than 100 and less than 500 candidates

Printed in the United Kingdom for HMSO
Dd300295 4/95 C130 G3397 10170